LEAD
WELL

LEAD WELL

*10 Steps to Successful and
Sustainable Leadership*

Ken Falke

COAUTHOR OF *STRUGGLE WELL: THRIVING IN THE AFTERMATH OF TRAUMA*

FOREWORD BY ARTHUR M. BLANK

LIONCREST
PUBLISHING

Lead Well

10 Steps to Successful and Sustainable Leadership

ISBN 978-1-5445-2418-4 *Hardcover*
      978-1-5445-2416-0 *Paperback*
      978-1-5445-2417-7 *Ebook*

TO MY FATHER
AND THE US NAVY FOR
SHAPING MY LEADERSHIP
PHILOSOPHY.

CONTENTS

FOREWORD

LEAD WELL

Arthur M. Blank
August 2021

I t was only a few minutes into my first meeting with Ken that I knew with certainty Ken and I were kindred spirits. We are both deeply committed to making the world a better place, a place of service above self and leaders focused on returning the many blessings we have received back into the world.

As our relationship has deepened, my respect and admiration for Ken has only grown. He is a kind, caring, and deeply thoughtful man who seeks to grow and learn every single day. Ken realizes the greatest form of philanthropy is providing people with the opportunity to live lives of passion, purpose, and service. Ken does this through his incredible work at the Boulder Crest Foundation and in the way he takes care of people.

Ken regularly asks himself the same questions I reflect on when I think about my family of businesses. Are we, as a company, worthy of our people's lives? Are we honoring the time, the commitment, and the life energy that they bring to their jobs every day?

The longest running study on the subject of satisfaction tells us that the good life is built on good relationships. I am convinced—as Ken is too—that the simple act of connecting to other human beings is the key to personal happiness and health, and building successful enterprises.

Far too often, leaders—overwhelmed by responsibilities at work and in their personal lives—forget a key maxim: a leader's primary job is to take care of their people. In Lead Well, Ken lays out ten ways you can do that, starting with learning how to lead yourself first.

It took me many years to learn an important lesson, one that Ken focuses on in detail in this book and in all areas of his life and work: if you can't find ways to refuel your own tank, your performance, in all areas of life, will suffer. Without the ability to lead yourself, you will struggle to be present and take the people you care about the most for granted.

As leaders, partners, parents, and grandparents, we can and must do better. Not only do the people that we lead deserve it, but so do we.

We live in a time of immense suffering, struggle, and stress. A time where the traditional walls between professional and personal have come crumbling down. A time where meetings occur virtually, with cameos from our children and pets. We have a responsibility to recognize that giving people a job isn't enough. We have to provide them with the opportunity to grow and contribute, and do so in a healthy and sustainable manner.

As leaders people entrust us with their most valuable asset—their time—it is incumbent on all of us in positions of authority and influence to step up to the task and take care of them. That starts by learning how to take care of yourself. I hope you will find this book as helpful as I have in providing guidance on the most effective ways to do that.

INTRODUCTION

Despite the fact that there are hundreds, if not thousands, of books on the subject of leadership, the truth is that good leaders remain far too rare. I have had the opportunity to work for a few great leaders and, unfortunately, many more toxic ones. A key reason why leadership proves so challenging for so many is that we overcomplicate things. Over the decades, I have developed a leadership philosophy that is simple, effective, and easy to understand and implement. Given how badly our country and world need good leaders, I feel it's time to share my philosophy in the hope that it will help you lead well, effectively supporting and guiding those you influence.

In the book *The Cathedral Within*, Bill Shore said the definition of leadership is simple: helping others get to a place they can't get to on their own. Leadership is a verb, not a noun, and requires action —lots of action. Leadership starts at home—with learning how to lead yourself first, and then applying a strategy this book presents to lead others. Great leadership is authentic, deeply personal, and sustainable.

I believe that the key to leading well comes down to ten timeless principles—The Lead Well 10—which I've successfully put into practice in the three major chapters of my life: the military, the business world, and as a philanthropist and nonprofit leader.

As a member of the US Navy's Explosive Ordnance Disposal (EOD) or bomb disposal community, I led small, highly trained teams on thousands of high-risk missions to disarm or safely detonate unexploded ordnance, landmines, and improvised explosive devices (IEDs). I made more than 1,000 parachute jumps and as many underwater dives during my twenty-one years of military service and served as an instructor at EOD schools in both the United States and the United Kingdom, responsible for training thousands of US and international military personnel in bomb disposal. In 2002, I retired as a Master Chief Petty Officer, the Navy's highest enlisted rank.

In the decade that followed, I became a serial entrepreneur. I founded two for-profit companies and two nonprofit organizations.

The first company, A-T Solutions, began in my garage in 2002, grew to 500 employees in eight years, won many awards, and became the world's leading provider of counter-terrorism training and consulting services for military and law enforcement personnel. The Secretary of Defense described A-T Solutions as a "national asset."

In 2004, early in the wars in Afghanistan and Iraq, my wife, Julia, and I started a small nonprofit called the Wounded EOD Warrior Foundation (today called the EOD Warrior Foundation), to help the most severely injured EOD personnel and their families. I ran the EOD Warrior Foundation until June of 2020, when my term as board chairman expired.

In 2008, we sold A-T Solutions, and all thirteen business partners became multi-millionaires. I continued to run the company for two and a half years—and by then a new mission was calling.

I had been spending a lot of time at military hospitals with severely wounded EOD personnel and their families. As I listened to their stories, I was inspired by their toughness and desire to get back on the battlefield. At about this time, the iPad hit the market. Our foundation started giving iPads to the severely wounded troops to help them better connect with their extended family members and their military units. After watching the joy in these virtual connections, I decided to start another company called Shoulder 2 Shoulder, with a mission of building an app to help facilitate these interactions more seamlessly. In late 2017, I sold my stock in Shoulder 2 Shoulder to my business partner.

After leaving Shoulder 2 Shoulder and the EOD Warrior Foundation, I decided to dedicate my life to serving as chairman of our second nonprofit: Boulder Crest Foundation, which Julia and I founded in 2011.

In 2010, Julia and I had begun hosting severely wounded EOD personnel and their families at our home in the Blue Ridge Mountains of Virginia, just an hour west of the military hospitals in the Washington, DC, area. After a year of having folks in our home, nearly every weekend, we decided to donate thirty-seven acres of our estate in early 2011 and build the nation's first privately funded wellness center dedicated solely to providing military veterans and first responders with a home away from home and respite from long hospital stays.

As I got to know these wounded warriors and their families better, I became fed up with what I saw as a broken mental healthcare system and was alarmed by a suicide epidemic among veterans and first responders. At Boulder Crest, our mission is to improve lives through innovative programs based on the science of Posttraumatic Growth. Today, Boulder Crest Foundation owns and operates beautiful, peaceful facilities in Bluemont, Virginia, and Sonoita, Arizona. In addition, we run the Boulder Crest Institute for Posttraumatic Growth. Boulder Crest Foundation currently employs thirty-five people, with an annual budget averaging $7 million.

Our work at Boulder Crest inspired the book *Struggle Well: Thriving in the Aftermath of Trauma*, which I co-authored with my good friend, Josh Goldberg. *Struggle Well* was written to share the Boulder Crest philosophy and offer a path of hope for all those who deal with afflictions such as anxiety, depression, addiction, and post-traumatic stress disorder (PTSD).

I've written *Lead Well* for a different audience. *Lead Well* is for those in leadership positions who want to improve and for those who are frustrated with bad leadership and hungry to grow and understand what effective leadership entails. *Lead Well* is not about business or business strategy. I'm talking about leadership in the broadest sense, whether you're leading yourself, your family, a business, a nonprofit, a community—or a nation.

The Lead Well 10 grew out of my own real-life and academic experiences in leadership—both as someone who has led and has been led by others, for better and worse. Two hundred and fifty thousand great people transition out of the military every year, and I believe the biggest reason they leave is bad leadership. This is the main reason I left the Navy too. This problem is not limited to the military. Studies consistently show that about 70 percent of Americans hate their jobs—and I believe what this really means is that they hate their bosses.

You won't find footnotes in this book, and I won't cite many studies. My philosophy of leadership is grounded in experience and academic learning. I earned my undergraduate degree in education and sociology through nineteen years of night school while serving in the Navy. I'm an alumnus of the Harvard Business School Executive Education program and hold a master's degree in Public Policy Management from Georgetown University. This year, I celebrate sixty years of leadership experience.

I have been privileged to sit with and learn from leaders including President George W. Bush; secretaries of Defense, State, and Homeland Security; the director of the FBI; several chairmen of the Joint Chiefs of Staff; US senators and congressmen; US and foreign ambassadors; the CEO of Ford Motor Company; the co-founders of the Home Depot; and many other amazing business leaders. Through my membership with the Young Presidents Organization (YPO), I am in contact with many CEOs in a continual learning environment.

No one who knew me as a teen would have foreseen where life has taken me. I entered the Navy as an angry young man in 1981 after barely graduating from high school and following a failed attempt to become a professional hockey player. My frustration generated a downward spiral of too much partying and too many fights. I was angry and something needed to change. I wanted to do something with meaning and purpose, so I headed to the recruiting office hoping to join the Army and become a Green Beret. The Army recruiting officer was at lunch. The Navy recruiting officer wasn't.

My hopes of becoming a US Navy SEAL ended with a failed eye exam. Instead, I was selected for the Navy's Ceremonial Guard, with duties ranging from serving at White House ceremonies to funerals at Arlington Cemetery. That was a first step in a new and better direction for me, a call to something higher. By the time I was recruited into the Navy's EOD community, my anger had subsided. I was a better person, capable of better things—an insight that's at the heart of the first of my leadership principles. You can't lead others to a place you have never been.

CHAPTER 1

LEAD WELL #1

Lead Yourself First

"We are builders of our own characters.
We have different positions, spheres, capacities, privileges,
different work to do in the world, different temporal
fabrics to raise; but we are all alike in this—
all are architects of fate."

—John Fothergill Waterhouse Ware

T he daily news is filled with stories of leaders who inflict their lack of wellness on others through inappropriate behavior. The consequences of their behavior can and do cripple the people and organizations they're leading. Unfortunately, I can tell you dozens of stories of unwell leaders I've encountered that prove the point.

That's why I begin the Lead Well 10 with this: *To lead others well, you have to be well.*

I believe that the first key to successful leadership is self-awareness, which leads to self-mastery. You must lead by example, not by living the life of "do as I say, not as I do." Unwell leaders let their egos get the best of them and adopt an egocentric, smarter- and holier-than-thou attitude that ultimately leads to a failure to treat others fairly.

No one is perfect; I understand that. But by leading yourself first and ensuring that you are the best role model possible—then owning your mistakes and failures—those you lead will be inspired to follow your example.

A CASE IN POINT

In the Navy, when a new officer takes command of a unit, the occasion is celebrated with a very traditional change of command ceremony. I attended one of these events along with my unit's commander toward the end of my career. The new commanding officer of one of our sub-units stood at the podium, telling everybody how great it felt to take command and build on the history of those who had come before him. He literally held the Holy Bible in his hand as he spoke of how Jesus had helped him and his family get to this point.

Weeks later, my commander called me into his office and closed the door. "Hey, boss," I said. "What's going on?"

"One of my commanding officers got arrested last night," he replied, "and I need some guidance from you."

"What happened?"

"He got arrested for soliciting a prostitute."

He didn't want to share the name, but I figured it out quickly. It was the guy who'd stood on the podium holding the Bible in his hand, thanking Jesus.

"What do you think I should do?" my commander said.

"Well," I replied, "what would you do if it was me? What would you do if it was a junior officer or an enlisted troop? Whatever you would do to them, I would expect you to do to this guy."

My commander's excuses followed: "He's eligible to make Captain, I don't want to ruin his career, I think I can cover it up and no one will find out."

Of course people found out. A friend in the CIA once told me that a secret is only kept between two people when one of them is dead. What the guy had done was completely wrong. He had not only broken civil law, but he had also violated the Uniform Code of Military Justice (UCMJ)—military law.

By the way, based on previous disciplinary actions my unit commander had taken, if the arrest had involved a junior officer or an enlisted troop, he would have hung them out to dry.

In the end, my commander swept the arrest under the table just the same. The guy who'd gotten arrested for soliciting a prostitute ultimately made the rank of Navy Captain and retired.

I was flabbergasted. Where was the accountability? What message did that send to everyone in the unit?

The best leaders lead by example. They don't say; they do. They don't tell; they show. They don't scream; they inspire. They aren't hypocrites; they are consistent. They don't lead from behind their desk; they lead by being a presence in the field or the shop floor.

Why? Because if you're saying one thing and doing another, everyone knows it. The people you're leading will see right through your bullshit, and I can guarantee that you will fail.

To lead well, you need to be well. This means the first person you need to lead well is yourself.

THE WELLNESS TRIANGLE

What does being well mean?

If you have read *Struggle Well*, you understand our Wellness Triangle philosophy already. If you haven't, you will find it and the science of Posttraumatic Growth covered extensively there. I won't cover it in the same depth in *Lead Well*, but here is an overview.

First, draw a triangle with three equal sides—your Wellness Triangle. Next, draw a circle in the center and ensure that the circle touches all three sides.

At the tip of the triangle, write the word Mind. On the bottom left point, write the word Body. On the bottom right point, draw a dollar sign—$. In the center of the circle inside the triangle, write the word Spirituality.

The outside of the triangle relates directly to our egos: how smart we are, how attractive we are, how much money we have. It's the "you" other people see. We all have an ego, and there's nothing wrong with that—so long as your ego is kept in check with a healthy dose of humility, optimism, and sense of accountability.

The triangle is one of the strongest geometric shapes, but even so it collapses if one side fails. That's why we need the circle of spirituality in the middle, holding everything up. Spirituality is the center of life; it touches all three sides of the triangle.

I'm not speaking strictly in a religious sense either. In the philosophy we teach at Boulder Crest, we define a healthy spirituality in three ways.

The first element of spirituality is your character. Are you the person you say you are? When you look at yourself in the mirror every morning, are you happy with what you see? Are you a leader who leads by example, or is it "Do as I say, not as I do"?

The second element of spirituality is your relationship to others. Are they based on mutuality? Do you have three to five friends you can turn to when you need help? Remember, as humans, we become the average of the three to five people we spend the most time with. Choose wisely!

The third element of spirituality is service. Are you engaged in service to others outside of your work? What are you doing for your neighbors? Your community? Your nation?

When you lead with a strong sense of spirituality, you become congruent—meaning your thoughts, feelings, and actions are all aligned in a positive way. Others will see that, admire it, and follow your lead.

Think of your circle in the center of your triangle as an exercise ball at the gym. If that ball is properly inflated, you can pretty much sit there and keep your balance for a long time. At its core, your Wellness Triangle is strong. But if that ball begins to deflate? Maybe your character or your relationships aren't what they should be; maybe your thoughts, feelings, and actions fall out of congruency. That's when leaders really start to struggle.

Worse yet, what if there's nothing in the center to begin with? Let's say you're an egomaniac, driven by the outside of your Wellness Triangle. Maybe your only relationships are the ones you buy. Perhaps you do nothing for anybody other than yourself. That's when pressure on one side or another of the triangle brings your life crashing down around you, and your capacity to lead with it.

THE PRESSURES OF LEADERSHIP

Put the sides and the circle together and you've got the strongest foundation in the world: the Wellness Triangle. But even the strongest triangle can be weakened under pressure—and the pressures of leadership are real. It's easy to envision a situation where the points of your Wellness Triangle flatten as a result.

In the eight years that I ran A-T Solutions, I gained fifty pounds. That wasn't who I'd been in the Navy, where I'd taken EOD trainees on runs so difficult that students remembered me as the guy who made them puke on the golf course run. I was spiritually well, mentally well, and financially well, but I was working sixteen- and seventeen-hour days, traveling more than two hundred days a year, and just didn't make time to take care of my body.

Every pound I gained after leaving the service was a measure of the burden I carried in building A-T Solutions—compounded by the burden of hiding the toll from others. I knew that when people see stress in their leader, they start to worry, and I didn't want anyone else to carry the load or see me becoming less well as a result of it. But who was I to think that fifty pounds could be hidden?

They say the top is a lonely place, and I was living that. But it was a mistake. My style today is much more collaborative. Now I know the power of relationships, openness, and honesty, and I am a better leader because of it. Leadership is really a relationship.

What happens when you're unwell? Your employees see right through it—and they start to question whether they're in the right place and working for the right person. Instead of growing your team members into leaders themselves, you lose them.

RECOGNIZING REALITY

As I said before, none of us are perfect, and leaders are no exception —though the worst leaders are prone to thinking they are. To be successful, we must focus on that reality, acknowledge it, accept it. Nobody is perfect. And if that's the case, the key to keeping your triangle strong has to begin with self-awareness. It can't end there—I was aware of my weight gain; I just couldn't bring myself to do anything productive about it—but change can't begin without awareness.

A great gauge for building self-awareness is measuring your Wellness Triangle frequently on a scale of 1 to 5 in each area, with 1 being the lowest score. If you give yourself 5's across the board, you're kidding yourself because—again—nobody's perfect. But by assessing ourselves honestly and setting short-term goals to improve our scores, we can all pursue perfection and improve our wellness over time.

The 1-to-5 scale is a subjective measuring tool, as you can imagine. I had a lot of skinny friends who were heavy drinkers and smokers, and even with my weight gain, I knew I was better off physically than they were.

How might you calibrate your scale? Here are my suggestions.

- **Mind:** If you're not sleeping, have a hard time thinking clearly, or just find putting one foot in front of the other very difficult, that's a 1. You may be over-medicated; you're not setting goals. Put those together and you're living the proverbial life of the tail wagging the dog—that could also be a 1. And a 5? You read, you meditate, you get eight hours of sleep every night. You wake up in the morning with a plan for the day, and if something goes wrong, you respond to it.

- **Body:** Let's say you're obese and can't bend over to tie your shoes; you can't walk up the stairs without getting out of breath. You consistently eat bad foods. You might be recovering from serious medical ailments or surgery; circumstances have bumped you down the scale. That's a 1. Now, let's say fitness is a part of your lifestyle. Maybe you're in the gym five to seven days a week, and you're working toward a goal, like a marathon or a triathlon. You are eating well, and your body is in great shape. That's a 5.

- **Finances:** If you're homeless, with no income, that's a 1. And a 5? At Boulder Crest, we tell people that doesn't have to mean you're a millionaire. Here's a more realistic standard: You've got a good job with a steady income, are spending less than you make, and have twelve to twenty-four months of cash flow covered in a savings account in case an emergency comes up—because they do. You have a plan and savings for retirement. That's a 5.

- **Spirituality:** If you are living a life with no core values, you have no healthy friendships, and you do nothing for anybody else, that's a 1. To be a 5, you have to be a person of character. You must understand the power of relationships and have your three-to-five healthy friends network, and, finally, you must be performing service for others. Every community in the world needs help. Are you involved?

BUILDING THE HABIT OF
SELF-AWARENESS

Building self-awareness is not a once-a-year, New Year's Resolution kind of thing. It's a daily task, and it begins with looking in the mirror every morning. Quite literally—for me, when I'm shaving.

No one likes to do it, at least not honestly. But it's important. I ask myself the same questions every time.

Where am I today? What can I do today to be a better version of myself? What must get done today to move the ball forward on my goals?

This exercise builds the internal dimension of self-awareness.

Self-awareness has an external dimension too. Don't let a meeting end without asking: "What can I do to make your job easier? What am I missing? I need you to tell me." Maybe you'd prefer to do it privately; if so, talk one-on-one with people you trust to tell you the truth. The point is recognizing that the person you see in the mirror may not be the person others see—or need—in their leader. And then you need to do something about it. Showing those you lead that you have a growth mindset, are hungry to change and grow, and are humble enough to take feedback is what walking the walk is all about. The alternative is destructive—to you, your organization, and those you lead. If you are well, you can lead well. If you aren't, you won't. Today I am fifty pounds lighter.

LEAD WELL #1:
Lead yourself first!

CHAPTER 2

LEAD WELL #2

Create and Clearly Communicate Your Vision

*"If you don't have a vision, you're going to
be stuck in what you know. And the only thing
you know is what you've already seen."*

—Iyanla Vanzant

One of the big challenges in the military is that officers transfer every two years, while the enlisted people may stay for up to five years. You'll get your commander's vision for your unit—we called it commander's intent—for two years, and that's it. On top of that, your new commander's intent is often different from the officer who came before, and normally different from the officer who follows. And, in their two years, they spend the first six months getting to know the unit and its troops and their last six months worrying about their next job.

Even worse, many times in my career, I was led by officers who never clearly articulated their vision for their tour of duty.

The result: There are no long-term plans for the future, and the lack of a clear and shared vision results in chaos. Middle managers develop their own vision, one that allows them to be successful in their job but may not align with what the leader wants to do.

When something goes wrong, everybody's blaming each other. The manager on the ground is just trying to do the right thing, but they don't have enough experience or perspective to draw on or a vision to follow. They have no chance and are destined either to skate by or fail.

When you receive no clear vision from the top, it's like getting in your car to go somewhere important without directions on how to get there. You end up just driving in circles.

No one comes to work wanting that. People want and need to feel fulfilled in their work. People take satisfaction in knowing that they're working toward a shared purpose. If they're simply showing up to collect a paycheck, your organization can't succeed. It's the leader's responsibility to prevent that—and that begins with defining and conveying your vision.

And that's the second principle to leadership in Lead Well: *Set and clearly communicate your vision.*

Speak it, write it, draw it. Keep it simple and make sure it's understood. Repeat it frequently. Everyone on your team must know where they are going and why. And I'm not suggesting that your vision is something on a tablet you hand down from on high. A good leader is curious, a teacher and a student, a constant learner—and that begins with how they go about developing a vision for their organization.

DEVELOPING A LIVING VISION

When you walk into a company where everyone fully understands what they're there to do, you can feel it right away. The energy, efficiency, and effectiveness are evident.

But you don't see that often enough. You're more likely to walk into a lobby, and there'll be a vision statement and core values posted on the wall—with everybody just walking by it. It's not engrained in the culture of the company. Employees don't even see it anymore. It might as well be taken down.

There's a difference between a vision and a vision that matters and is understood. Clear vision begins with how it's developed: collectively.

A good leader doesn't simply walk around the office, handing out their vision, posting it on the wall. It's not just you as a leader declaring, "This is my vision!"

Good leaders sit down with their management team and say, "Hey, here's what I'm thinking." They foster a conversation, a real give and take. True collaboration is what you need to create a vision that matters. In a small organization, this can involve most if not all your team. In a big organization, it involves your management team, which must be in tune with the broader organization.

And that work never stops. You need to be willing to challenge and change your own vision too.

Ever since my first company, the process we've followed involves gathering the management team at an offsite meeting every fall. Today at Boulder Crest, we have thirty-five employees, and fourteen of us join in the annual offsite. In the month before we meet, every manager sits with their teams to get their input on a SWOT analysis: a worksheet that lays out strengths, weaknesses, opportunities, and threats from their point of view.

When the managers gather, we begin by looking at our vision and asking, "Is this still where we're going? Is this really what we believe in and want to do as a team? Can you get up every day excited about going to work and be satisfied in understanding our mission and the role you're playing in helping us get there?"

Having revisited our vision, the managers assess what we've accomplished in the year so far and what remains to be done.

Out of those conversations, we adjust our vision if we need to, and from there, we create our new three-year strategic plan, with very specific goals for the upcoming year.

You need to think of your vision as a living thing. In so many organizations, it's much less than that. I've done some consulting with small businesses that wrote their vision statement along with their business plan ten years ago, and they haven't looked at it since. Their employees have no idea what lies in the dust-covered book.

In Boulder Crest's ten years, we have changed our vision once and tweaked it five or six other times. As we've grown and evolved, we've fundamentally changed what we do at Boulder Crest—and so our vision has evolved too.

You can find many books and articles about writing vision and mission statements and developing business plans. Don't get hung up on flowery and obscure language. At the core of all this advice is this: make it short and clear, and ensure that everyone fully understands it.

COMMUNICATE YOUR VISION SO OTHERS NEVER LOSE SIGHT OF IT

Your vision must be understood and communicated like a drumbeat. That drumbeat leads to success. It's not a question of set it and forget it, which only leads to failure.

Once every year at Boulder Crest we publish what we call the Boulder Crest Way. It's not an electronic document, but an actual handbook that's nicely printed and distributed to everyone. The handbook is different from our employee manual, although there's some duplication.

The handbook begins at the highest level: with our vision statement, followed by our mission statement. (The mission statement is an ambitious and more specific statement than the vision statement. It's a step toward action. The two are related, but different.)

From there it goes into our one-year goals and how much money we have to raise in that year to support the organization. We include some inspirational quotes too.

We kick off each year with an all-hands meeting in January, where we present what we accomplished in the previous year, what rolled over and why, and the new goals we've developed. The meeting is designed to make clear that the goals were developed by the management team, their supervisors, and not just me. If we've decided not to pursue a particular goal that came up in the SWOT analysis, we explain why. We ask for questions on anything that's unclear and comments on anything that anyone feels strongly about that didn't make the year's goals. When the conversation is over, I close by saying, "Okay. I'm going to consider that buy-in on our new goals, all around."

That's not the end of communicating our vision. It's just the beginning.

Every month, we do an all-hands call. I know this can be challenging for a big organization, but we are small enough that we can all get together on a call. As managers, we talk *with* every employee, not *at them.*

During that meeting, I'll remind everybody of our vision: remember, this is what we're here to do. Every time; it's that important. For us to succeed, the members of our team have to work with a clear sense of direction. They need to understand why they're there and feel that they're contributing to the cause. To me, that's what it's all about.

BOULDER CREST'S 2021 VISION AND MISSION STATEMENTS

Vision

Boulder Crest Foundation's vision is a world where all combat veterans, first responders, and their families have the training, skills, and support they need to transform their struggling into lifelong Posttraumatic Growth.

Mission

Our mission is to facilitate Posttraumatic Growth through transformative programs, world-class training and education initiatives, and research and advocacy efforts.

A TALE OF TWO VISIONS

Here's a story that illustrates why I'm so passionate about developing an effective, living vision. In the early to mid-nineties, the Navy came out with a strategic vision document for the EOD community in which I served: here are the missions we support, here are the mission areas we're going to be proficient in, and so forth. It was a pretty big document, running nearly eighty pages, and I'll say a few things about it:

- It was a pretty good document, clear, and useful.

- It was never shared with the majority of the EOD community.

- It was created in a vacuum.

If you were a Navy EOD troop who did read it, you'd have said, "This is pretty good—and I wish I'd seen it earlier in my career."

I spent my last stint in the Navy in the West Coast headquarters for the EOD community. When I got there in 1999, the document hadn't been updated in several years. We were charged with the rewrite. That document went back and forth between the West and East Coast headquarters for more than a year as we worked our way through it.

Two things happened as a result. One, it never got officially published. And two, we killed a lot of morale and manpower.

Within the last year, the Navy *finally* published a new strategic vision for the EOD community. And I've noticed on social media that they've shared the document, or at least the unclassified version of it, with everyone in the community. I've seen a lot of discussion of it there. It's too early to say whether it's making a difference, but they've taken an entirely different approach in sharing—and a better one too.

But it's twenty years later. Twenty years that members of the EOD community spent in the midst of a massive war, full of bombs, pursuing their very sophisticated, life-or-death mission without really understanding the bigger picture.

In the civilian world, the stakes are different—but developing and communicating a living vision for your team is no less important. Too many companies just stick you in a cubicle. You don't really know the person on your left or your right. You're not really clear on the bigger picture of what the company's all about. You're just whacking away on your keyboard, getting in your eight hours, and collecting your paycheck. It doesn't build loyalty; it doesn't build satisfaction; it leads to nothing but turnover.

Visions that don't serve as a real and meaningful guide to action are destined to fail and are detrimental to employee satisfaction. It shouldn't be that way.

LEAD WELL #2:

Create and clearly communicate your vision!

CHAPTER 3

LEAD WELL #3

Set and Achieve Goals that Align with Your Vision

*"Our goals can only be reached through a
vehicle of a plan, in which we must fervently believe,
and upon which we must vigorously act.
There is no other route to success."*

—Pablo Picasso

I f you want to lose fifty pounds, don't try to lose fifty pounds. That's your destination—your vision for wellness. Try to lose two pounds in a week instead. That's a waypoint—your initial goal. Once you achieve it, then set a new goal: lose two more pounds the next week too.

If you don't set personal goals, you'll end up living the life of the proverbial dog wagged by its tail. The same is true of your organization. If you do regularly set goals, you will also join some rarified air; only 3 percent of people in the world regularly set goals, and they are light-years more successful than their counterparts in the 97 percent.

So that's Lead Well #3: *Set and achieve goals that align with your vision.*

DEFINING A GOAL

As a leader, the vision you develop with your team defines where you're going as an organization. The goals you develop next define how you're going to get there and should be focused on results. They clarify the steps you need to take to establish the momentum that can carry you to your objectives as an organization.

How are you going to lose two pounds? Eat less. Move more.

THE CHARACTERISTICS OF A MEANINGFUL GOAL

Goals are actionable. They create milestones for success and provide the satisfaction that comes with accomplishing something. It works the other way too: when you fall short of your goals, it highlights the need to stop and reassess.

Goals are measurable. There's a saying that you can't manage what you don't measure, and you can't improve on things you're not managing. Without measurable goals, you can't hold yourself or others accountable, and that's critical in accomplishing goals.

Goals should be short term. By that I mean a year or less. In our planning process at Boulder Crest, we set lofty goals for three years, specific and actionable goals for the year, and measure our progress on our one-year goals every month. The level of accountability built into our system is high. We've either met a due date or we haven't; if something hasn't been completed, we'll talk about the adjustments we need to make. Do we need to change direction? Detour for gas?

These discussions aren't about blaming. They're about solving. In a monthly meeting, I might say, "In October of last year, you thought this was a two-month project. What's changed? Are you too busy? Caught up in something else that's not in our strategic plan?" Perhaps it's just taken a little longer than expected; in that case, we can change the due date in the plan.

As a leader, you can nail your vision and do a great job of communicating it—but if you fall short on defining goals that are achievable over the short term and measurable, you'll end up with an organization that's not meeting its objectives.

THE NOT-TO-DO LIST

An effective employee translates their goals into a daily task list: the working steps they'll take today toward achieving them. The problem with to-do lists is that in many cases, they either get too long or don't actually align with the goals they're trying to achieve.

I'll sometimes tell people I see struggling with this that they're better off figuring out what they shouldn't do that day, rather than what they should. What goes on the not-to-do list? The things that prevent you from feeling like you're an important part of the team, working toward its common purpose. Personal things can creep in that don't align with the organization's needs. Rather than creating more things for ourselves to do, we're often better off asking what's holding us back from being more effective and efficient.

THE SMART METHODOLOGY

I'm a believer in the SMART methodology for setting effective goals. It is straightforward and encapsulates what we've been talking about. We've developed a goal-setting worksheet with each element written down on it. This may seem over-scripted, but once you become familiar with the checklist, it becomes second nature.

SMART goals are...

- **Specific:** A specific goal is granular and clear.

- **Measurable:** If you can't measure your progress, you don't know where you are.

- **Action-Oriented:** You can't say you're going to cure cancer tomorrow. You might want to, but an action-oriented goal is something you can actually do and see results from.

- **Realistic:** A realistic goal is tied to the vision and mission of your organization.

- **Time-Specific:** It's got a deadline for when it has to be accomplished.

THE TRUE MEASURE OF HARD WORK

You can fool yourself into thinking that the length of your to-do list is the measure of how hard you are working. The symptoms of this problem are easy to spot: another aimless meeting, dead-end tasks, pointless paperwork.

The true measures of hard work are the outcomes.

I worked with a guy at my first company who thought that if he was at work when I was at work, that meant he was working hard and that I'd be impressed. I'd often approach him and ask what he was working on. His answers were always vague. "Well," he'd say, "I've just got a couple things I've got to do."

I could tell he wasn't there for the right reasons. The more we talked, the more I realized that he believed spending time with me was more important than getting things done. That's when I had a long conversation with him.

I learned to tell everybody in my company that, personally, I got more done from six to eight in the evening than during the rest of the day—because those were the only times when people weren't coming into my office. Nobody else needed to be in the office at six to eight at night; they should be home, proud of what they accomplished during the day.

I'd also tell people that if they had nothing to do, do it somewhere else. Our company was filled with teammates who traveled a lot, all over the world, in the course of doing their jobs. Their work could take them away from their families for extended periods. If they found themselves at work without a lot to do one day, I didn't want them in the office sitting around and telling stories. I wanted them to go home and spend time with their family. That was always our philosophy and the way we built our culture.

THE LEADER'S ROLE
AROUND GOALS

As I've described, we revisit our vision and mission and develop our goals for the year in an annual offsite meeting involving the management team. It's not my plan we're executing; it's the team's plan, and everyone has bought into it. Normally we'll emerge with a handful of major goals for the year, with a half-dozen or so minor goals listed beneath each of them, making explicit the milestones we need to achieve to deliver on our major goals and fulfill our mission and vision.

Here's an example: For 2021, we set a major goal of creating a new website. Beneath it were the minor goals we needed to succeed, such as interviewing multiple companies for bids, evaluating the bids based on creativity and value, creating a tiger team within the company to oversee the creation of the new site, and presenting it to me for approval before it goes live. The milestones are all quite clear and very much spelled out.

I chair our monthly accountability meetings, where we review the progress toward all our goals. If we're falling behind, we adjust as I've described. I don't wait for the monthly meetings for trouble to surface either. I like to check in weekly with our team leaders to see if we are on track.

Leaders know they need to be communicating with me too. Everyone knows that if they're facing challenges with completing goals, they shouldn't wait until the management meeting to tell me. Our managers operate on what we call a three-strike principle. If I'm just learning something's behind on the day it's due, that's a strike. (Failing to achieve a goal isn't a strike; failing to raise the issue in time to address it is.) Managers get three strikes. Get a fourth and you don't have to leave the company—but you do have to leave the management team. To date, we've never had a manager get even one strike.

A key part of this goes back to the first principle of leading well. If you are well and approachable, you can create a culture where people are comfortable acknowledging that they are behind schedule, have too much on their plate, or need more support or guidance. I work hard to create open lines of communication because it provides for transparency and openness, and prevents blaming and shaming.

It's different, of course, if you have five hundred employees, and different again if you have five thousand. But I am confident that this approach is scalable. Now you're working with a management team that represents a much smaller percentage of the organization as a whole. What's more challenging for the leader is ensuring that every division in the company is working toward success as defined in their shared vision—and then ensuring that vision is passed down through all the layers of the organization to the people in the cubicles who are actually doing the work.

LEAD WELL #3:
Set and achieve goals that align with your vision!

CHAPTER 4

LEAD WELL #4

Listen Well

*"Most of the successful people I've known are the
ones who do more listening than talking."*

—Bernard Baruch

B ack in 1999, while I was stateside in the Navy, we deployed
an explosives disposal team onboard the *USS Belleau Wood*
off the coast of East Timor, in Southeast Asia, in the midst of an
international military skirmish. The only vehicles on board for the
team were Humvees, the Jeep of our day, with its familiar bulky
shape and wide wheelbase. But the roads in East Timor were very
narrow, and that wide stance meant the Humvees might bottom

out with their wheels in the ditches on either side and get stuck.

If that happens when you're under fire, it's a very bad thing.

I had just done an exchange tour with British forces in Bosnia, who were equipped with Land Rovers and Mercedes-Benz vehicles that were perfectly suited to missions in small countries with primitive roads, like East Timor.

I raised what to me was an important issue in a meeting back home. When we deploy our teams to small countries like East Timor, I said, we need to reassess our vehicle allocations to make sure they're properly equipped.

A senior officer in the room jumped me. "We can't do that," he said. He didn't ask me about the situation on the ground in East Timor, or Bosnia either, for that matter. He didn't show any interest in hearing me out. "We have an allotment from the Navy," he said. "It is what it is. We can't change it."

What he was saying wasn't true, and it wasn't fact-based either. But he felt the need to spew—to give a firm and decisive answer before he understood the issue I had raised, without the experience I brought to the discussion, and without showing any interest in the concern I had raised or exploring the options for addressing it.

Thank God the bullets weren't flying at our guys in East Timor, stuck on a road in a vehicle that wouldn't move.

Managers push paper, leaders push people—and that has to begin with listening to them. Effective listening is the basis of effective action. It starts with clear communication and valuing opinions, which means listening and observing before you open your mouth. Listen to understand, not to just reply.

So that's Lead Well #4: *Listen well.*

WE'RE WIRED TO ACT

I wish I could call the officer's reaction unusual. It's not. My experience in many situations—in the military, in the business world, in nonprofits—has shown me that most humans are quick to judge and give advice. Sometimes they have the best of intentions. I work with a woman now who calls herself a fixer—and that's just what she is. Whenever an issue comes up, she jumps straight to fixing it.

"What can I do?" she says.

"Let's discuss it first," I answer. "We'll figure out what we need to do during our conversation."

Even the military, where decisions can be matters of life and death, recognizes the wisdom in not rushing to solutions. "Slow is smooth," the saying goes, "and smooth is fast."

Saying the right words is one thing. Honoring them is another. In reality, people in all walks of life are very quick to want to live other people's lives and "fix" their problems. They're eager to provide you with solutions, whether they've got the understanding or the experience to support their advice or not. Maybe it's financial advice, marital advice, job advice. We've all heard it, and maybe we've given it too.

I'm a firm believer in the philosophy that we should not provide advice without the experience to back it up. Going through life any other way is dangerous. It perpetuates a lack of learning, a failure to slow down, clarify, and really understand. We live in a country where misinformation is proliferating at a pace impossible to keep up with. I call it the "sound-bite" nation. We don't stop to ask questions because we prefer to keep moving, always—and we just make other people's mistakes over and over again.

LEADERS WHO DON'T LISTEN

Leaders who are unwell and lack self-awareness are prone to a dangerous assumption. They think they're the smartest person in the room. That *could* be true—but if it was always so in the past, it certainly is not anymore. Technology has leveled the playing field when it comes to knowledge. There is much more knowledge in your cellphone than anyone can hold in their brain. Today the most junior person in the room has access to information that enables them to get answers to questions instantly.

Leaders who lack self-awareness are also prone to the belief that they can solve all problems. No one can. I'm sixty years old now, with a pretty vast background in leading others—and there are lots of things I'm not an expert in. I love cars, and always have. That doesn't mean I'm a mechanic. I can recommend a great mechanic, but I'm not the guy to fix your car.

Effective leaders don't begin with answers. They begin with listening—and they do it well.

ATTENTIVE LISTENING

The signs of someone who's not truly listening are easy to see. I start by watching their lips while I'm speaking. Some people are in such a rush to give an answer or share their opinion that their brain has their lips moving before you even finish speaking, and oftentimes, talking over you.

The second tell is what comes out of their mouth first. Is it advice? Then you can tell they're not a good listener because they haven't fed back what you're saying in a way that shows they've absorbed it.

A third clue: inattention. Are they on their phone, sending a quick text? Are their eyes on you or the ground?

There is a better way of communicating: attentive, active listening. An attentive listener is engaged and paying attention to what's being said. They're giving their undivided attention to the speaker.

If you think of it from a military perspective, it's like using a two-way radio, which is both a transmitter and a receiver. If you and the person you're talking to both hold the transmit button down at the same time, nobody would ever hear each other. Somebody's got to transmit, and somebody's got to receive. When you're done transmitting, you say, "Over," and release the button. If the person on the other end understands, they'll push the transmit button and reply, "Roger." If they don't understand, they will say, "Say Again."

Attentive listening begins with giving the person you're talking with your undivided attention and showing them that you're listening with the message you send when it's your turn to transmit.

"Do I understand that you…?"

"Can you tell me more about…?"

"So is this what you mean by…?"

"Can you clarify one thing…?"

Those are signals of attentive listening. When an attentive listener does speak, they're more likely to begin with a question than an opinion.

Attentive listening also requires resisting the very, very human temptation to interrupt. This takes patience that doesn't always come easily; you've got a meeting to get to or someplace else you need to be. Being a good listener means yielding the floor *and* your own agenda until you've heard the other person out. The only reason to interrupt is to seek clarity: "We've been talking for the last ten minutes, and I want to make sure I'm understanding you before we go any further."

COMMUNICATION IS A
TWO-WAY STREET

When they do speak, an attentive listener begins by asking questions to make sure they understand what the other person is trying to say. And when they do make a decision, offer advice, or ask the other person to do something, the attentive listener makes sure that they are clearly understood as well. That can begin with a question too: Are you clear on what I said? Can you play it back to me? Where do we go from here?

This is true even in an emergency situation. I was in an airport once and running behind when a stranger passed out right in front of me. Several of us stopped to help him. I turned to a person standing by and said, "Can you call 9-1-1?" Then the stranger who passed out began to stir. "Do I still need to call 9-1-1?" the bystander asked. "Yes," I said. "Do you have a cell phone? Do you know how to call 9-1-1?"

My point in telling this story is that even when you're in an emergency and the conversation is going back and forth very quickly, clarity is everything. When people get excited and panic, they can forget what to do.

Always play it back. An attentive conversation is built on back and forth. It is a two-way process. Whether you are going to act on something you've learned in conversation or not, you must be clear in your response.

THE EFFECTS OF
ATTENTIVE LISTENING

Attentive listening builds confidence in others. It gives the person you are speaking with the feeling that they are important, that they are being understood, and that they have the ability in many cases to come up with a solution themselves. Sometimes simply being heard is enough; we all want to feel listened to.

As a leader, that's one of your objectives in conversation: the other person understands that they've been heard, and they feel good about that. The objective is that if there's action to be taken as a result of the conversation, the listener fully understands the issue at hand and what's to be done about it. That doesn't necessarily mean that you have the absolute answer. You might say: "I hear you loud and clear, and I need to think about it. Let's talk again tomorrow." Or: "Here are some initial thoughts. Would any of these make things better?"

Sometimes you'll have to disappoint the other person at the end of the conversation. It's inevitable. Attentive listening ensures that, when you're in that situation, you can share your decision with the confidence that you truly understand where they're coming from and can meet them in that place.

THE POWER
OF BEING HEARD

I moved into the nonprofit world at the height of the war in Afghanistan, at a time when a lot of American servicemen and women were
coming home as amputees. As part of helping these soldiers and
their families, I would sit by their beds and listen to their stories.
And I never once talked to a wounded soldier—even a quadruple
amputee—who didn't want to go back to Afghanistan. They had a
dream, even while they were laying in a hospital bed healing, that
where they really belonged was back with their comrades, fighting
this war—whether they had the physical ability to do it or not.

And it wasn't up to me to tell them that they couldn't do that anymore. My role was to sit and listen to them talk about the good
times and the memories that were created during those deploy-
ments. They didn't want me to feel sorry for them for what they
were going through, lying there in the hospital bed. Given the
opportunity, the choice, they would do it again. They just wanted
to be heard.

That's when I really began to understand the value of listening.
Because of my experience, they could talk to me about the details
of the fight. They could talk to me about where they wanted to
be because I had been there too—and then they could talk to me

about the challenges their families might be having, challenges that my organization was there to help them face. Was that leading by listening? In a sense, it was.

> **Managers push paper, leaders push people –**
> **and that begins with listening to them.**

CHAPTER 5

LEAD WELL #5

Lead with Kindness

W hen Julia and I reached the point in life where we were ready to have a family, we had difficulty conceiving. When she did get pregnant, we were filled with joy—tempered, of course, with concern for her health and that of our baby.

At the time, we were stationed in Virginia Beach, and I was scheduled for a six-month shipboard deployment halfway through her pregnancy. In the meantime, I was due to be trained in deep-sea diving along with others in my unit for three months at the diving school in Panama City, Florida—meaning nine months in total away from home.

The Navy had a deep-sea diving school in Virginia Beach too, and it was regarded as the toughest.

I approached my Master Chief to see if I could do my training in Virginia Beach rather than going to Panama City with everyone else. I explained that I wanted to support my pregnant wife as best I could.

"Sailor, if you're looking for sympathy from me," the Master Chief said, "you will find it in the dictionary—between shit and syphilis."

My first thought was, did that really just come out of this guy's mouth? But his view was that if the Navy says this is what you're going to do, it's what you're going to do.

"I'm not really looking for sympathy, Master Chief," I said. "I'm just looking for an opportunity to be home a little bit more because I'm deploying. If I have to go to Florida, I'll go to Florida."

That's not the end of the story. The Master Chief left the posting just a few days later, and a new Master Chief stepped into his place. I approached him too.

"Absolutely," he said, after hearing me out. "We'll make it happen." And he did. His view was, if it makes sense, and he can do right by one of his sailors in the process, then it was worth making it work.

I tell this story to illustrate Lead Well #5: *Lead with kindness.*

TONE IS CONTAGIOUS

If you feel that every time you bring a problem or concern to an authority figure—your parents, your boss—the answer is going to be no, then you tend not to bring things forward. When we don't have the opportunity to engage with our leaders and seek support and guidance, small problems and concerns fester—and become big problems. Chaos and frustration ensue.

But when you work for people who are open to these discussions and are good listeners, the opposite is true. You want to bring your questions and concerns to them, before issues get out of hand—so your organization thrives, and your people do too. When people see that their leader brings passion to the cause and shows kindness toward others, it sets a positive, infectious tone.

I mean "infectious" in a very positive and concrete way. For most humans, we become the product of our training in life, beginning in early childhood at the hands of parents, teachers, relatives, and friends. The learning never stops. If you're spending time with people who are kind, that tends to rub off. Kindness ripples from person to person in any environment, including the workplace. The same is true of spending time with toxic people.

Which approach to leadership is more common? As I've mentioned, surveys of workplace satisfaction in America regularly show that 70 percent of employees hate their jobs. More than half of employees said that their employer never asked them how they were doing in the midst of the COVID-19 pandemic. And the average turnover rate of employees in America is nearly 45 percent. The answer is clear. People don't leave companies; they leave people.

RESPONDING, NOT REACTING

One thing we teach at Boulder Crest is the difference between responding and reacting. We see it as an important distinction, and we describe this philosophy extensively in *Struggle Well*.

We define a response as thoughtful and conscious, and a reaction as just the opposite: a knee-jerk impulse. A response is positive, a reaction negative. We view them as a choice. Whether a decision has to be made rapidly—such as during an emergency or crisis—or if there's time to think it through, you always have the ability to either respond or react. With training and experience comes the ability to respond faster.

In some situations, the consequences of making the wrong choice—reacting rather than responding—can be a matter of life and death. In the Navy, we had a diver who got tangled in a rope with a weight at the bottom. In a panic, he cut the rope above his head. The weight took him to the bottom of the ocean, never to be seen again. He was a good diver too—but his reaction was the wrong choice, and it proved fatal.

This is a choice that leaders face too, all the time, even if no one's life is on the line. Effective leaders never react. They respond. And again, that tone is contagious.

THE CONSEQUENCES
OF A SCREAMER

At some point, whether the result of personal or professional challenges, we get the chance to see how the people we work with react to stress. It may not be obvious early on, but eventually we see their true colors. How leaders handle stress is one key way to sort the great ones from the not-so-good ones. A leader who responds under stress, instead of reacting, conveys the reassuring feeling that you're on the right team—that we're not in panic mode, regardless of what's happening.

On the other hand, some leaders create stress. I call them screamers, and a screamer always screams. It may not be verbal, and that doesn't matter. When someone is screaming on the inside, others can see it. They may sweat or curse under their breath; I once had a boss who calmed himself down at the end of the day with a few drinks at his desk before driving home drunk.

Screaming is contagious too. Screamers draw others into their behaviors, whether it's as dark as drinking in strip bars before going home to your family or as seemingly positive as buying expensive bicycles and going for long rides, because in the workplace they reward those who kiss their ass and play along while shunning those who don't. They're impulsive and rash, and that makes others uncomfortable. Unchecked, they'll drive good people away and turn the rest of their team toxic.

WHAT KINDNESS MEANS

What does kindness mean in the context of leadership? First and foremost, it means leading with compassion for others. By that I mean demonstrating that people come first. If they understand the mission and vision, they get things done, and done right. But if you put the mission and vision ahead of the people, dragging them rather than leading them, they'll resist. It's human nature. Leading with kindness means coaching and providing the support and guidance others need from you to succeed in their jobs.

Finally, kindness means leading with an awareness that you are there to serve the interests of the organization as a whole, not a minority—and certainly not a minority of one, yourself. An organization as a whole embodies many different values and points of view, likes and dislikes, and you can't impose yours on others. The people who make up your organization are its most important element. When you put "me" into the equation, others see right through it, and it's a recipe for disaster.

WHAT KINDNESS DOESN'T MEAN

What leading from kindness *doesn't* mean is also important. It doesn't mean that employees get a free ride. They need to be held accountable for their actions. Sometimes the kindest thing you can do is share honest feedback with someone who isn't a good fit so they have the opportunity to start over at another organization. The same holds true for falling short of their goals at a certain point. You'll find that holding others and yourself accountable is contagious too, provided—as always—that you respond, not react, when things don't go according to plan.

At Boulder Crest, we detail the core values of our organization in the first pages of our team handbook: integrity, selflessness, mission-focused, empathy, courage, and growth-oriented. We put them in the employee agreement too. And we make clear that if you don't live up to these values, and they aren't values that you embrace, then this isn't the place for you to work and that's okay.

LEADING FROM PASSION

I hate the concept of motivational speakers because I've always believed that motivation and passion have to come from within. Finding your passion—the "why" that gives meaning and purpose to our lives—is one of the most challenging aspects of the journey. Obviously, I'm not talking here about being passionate about your favorite football team or hobby. I'm talking about that sense of internal satisfaction and fulfillment that comes from waking up every day with the belief that we are part of something bigger than ourselves and are making a real difference in the world.

The "why" in your life changes with your circumstances and your age. Some of the teenagers who play electric guitar in a band make a life of it, but most move on.

The root of passion is learning to love yourself. Many people who struggle to find passion are so out of touch with themselves that they simply can't connect with what drives them. Their lives are like a scene from the movie *Groundhog Day*: wake up, go to work, come home, and do it all over again. This is a recipe for despair and misery, and is what life looks like when the tail wags the dog.

THE IMPLICATIONS OF PASSION

First, like kindness, passion is contagious. People who see a genuine sense of passion in their leader are motivated by it and learn from it. The leader's first responsibility is to act from a deeply passionate place. If the leader can't connect to their why, how could anyone working for them do so? When the leader exudes passion, it provides the inspiration that helps others motivate themselves.

Some will say that you can't teach passion, and perhaps that's true, in an academic sense. But as a leader, you also have a responsibility to talk about and demonstrate your passion, and to ensure that the people in your organization have the opportunity to find and act from theirs. That begins with giving them a sense of purpose in their work, and then encouraging them by helping them grow and forge connections with others. Most people will behave like those who inspire them, and the converse is true as well.

Even when you have an organization like Boulder Crest, dedicated to helping people change their lives for the better, you've got to pull people out of their comfort zones and create passion projects. When the trauma of COVID-19 hit, we looked inside ourselves as an organization, just as we teach the veterans and first responders we serve to do. We set out to grow and become a better version of ourselves. Our staff set out to do food and clothing drives for people who were struggling. We bought extras from a paper towel and toilet paper factory and delivered them to foster homes and a shelter for abused women. Even as COVID-19 brought normal life to a halt, we didn't feel paralyzed. We felt energized.

PUTTING IT ALL TOGETHER

As a leader, when you start to assemble the elements we've been talking about in this chapter, you foster a sense of community based on a shared purpose that brings joy and satisfaction to the people in your organization. It begins with a clear vision about where the organization is going, which establishes a sense of purpose, and it's built by rewarding those who contribute to the mission in positive ways while holding those who don't accountable. Leaders who act out of kindness and their own sense of passion, who respond but don't react in even the most stressful moments, create the types of organizations that others *want* to work for—without ever needing to scream, on the inside or out.

> An effective leader says what they mean,
> means what they say—and doesn't act out of a
> spirit of meanness toward others.

CHAPTER 6

LEAD WELL #6

Hire Quality People

"I'm convinced that nothing we do is more important than hiring and developing people. At the end of the day you bet on people, not on strategies."

—Lawrence Bossidy

During my years in the Navy, two friends of mine earned PhDs while they were on active duty. Both did dissertations on the validity of the entry exam you take when you enlist in the military. It's called the ASVAB—it stands for the Armed Services Vocational Aptitude Battery—and the result is your ASVAB score.

The ASVAB scale goes from zero to one hundred, and fifty is the mean. Most test-takers score between thirty and seventy.

To have the opportunity to do certain jobs in the military, you need to achieve a certain score; if you're above average, maybe you can be an electronics technician on a jet. If you're well above average and in the Navy, maybe you can go into nuclear power. Your opportunities are based on this proficiency test.

My friends' dissertations both focused on the EOD community, which also required a high score. They came at the question in two different ways—and both concluded that ASVAB scores had no direct correlation to successfully graduating from training as an EOD technician. Their findings were complex—these were dissertations, after all—but distilled down to their essence, what they found was that an individual's motivation was a much better indicator of success than their academic scores.

I tell this story not to trash the military's ASVAB test, but to illustrate the challenge leaders face in acting on Lead Well #6: ***Hire quality people.***

I've always believed that with the right people, you can accomplish any mission. And that begins with hiring. Other things matter too, but hiring comes first.

THE THREE QUESTIONS

At Harvard Business School, where I studied executive leadership, we learned a simple concept: hire for attitude, train for skills. When recruiting, elite military units turn the same concept into three questions.

- Can they do the job?

- Will they do the job?

- Are they a good fit?

The first of these questions relates to things like technical expertise and physical abilities. Obviously, you need fine motor skills to be in the bomb disposal business. If your hands shake, no amount of motivation can qualify you for this work.

But the second question is all about motivation. Does this person have the motivation required to understand, learn, and do the job? Will they come to work every day with the fortitude required to complete the tasks they're given? It's all about will, and not everyone has it.

The third question is about culture, which in organizational terms, I define culture as how we get things done. Leaders establish culture —and to succeed on a team, its members need to be cultural fits.

The same is true in the business world. In my mind, there are three basic types of organizations: entrepreneurial startups, which have to move fast; established companies, which are process-oriented; and bureaucratic organizations, where there's not a lot of room for innovation or changes in processes and policies. Each of these organizations has a different culture and requires different types of people.

If you take a person with entrepreneurial instincts and put them in an assembly line, it's not a good fit. If you take someone who thrives in a stable, process-driven environment and put them into a startup, they won't be a good fit either.

As a leader, I always felt that it was the team's role to find out if an applicant can and will do the job. My role is to focus on fit. The team's opinion on that question is important too, of course, but I see it as my primary responsibility in the hiring process.

The bigger the organization, the more important it is to bring in people who don't disrupt your culture. That doesn't mean they can't bring in new and different ideas, or that people have to comply or just be good at following orders. Great employees question the status quo, and that is important. But the way they bring in their ideas is critically important. Generally speaking, people don't like change. When a new person joins a team where things are going well, and from day one offers recommendations about different ways of working, the team that's already in place will resist it. That's why it's so important to evaluate for fit in the hiring process—and to instill your organization's values in the people who join it.

As an organization grows, its leader can't be involved in every hire, but it's a critical responsibility and one that hiring managers must fully understand. After all, you can't lead a team without teammates.

When I left A-T Solutions, we had 500 employees—and I had been actively involved in hiring about 400 of them. In a company with 100,000 employees, the CEO can't come close to participating in every hire. In that case, it's about instilling your values around hiring in the people who make those decisions so they understand what to look for.

SELECTING FOR QUALITY

I think of selection as the process of recruiting, interviewing, and hiring. At Boulder Crest, the three questions—can they do the job, will they do the job, and are they a good fit?—are central to our process, and as I've said, motivation is critical. On that subject, don't overrate the resume.

In *Struggle Well*, we told the story of a friend and Master Chief Navy SEAL who was involved in their selection process. He told me the people who were most likely to make it through SEAL training weren't the ones with the sterling resumes and the great natural abilities—the star quarterbacks and water polo players in high school. They'd never been yelled at, never dealt with adversity; their egos tended to make them great individual contributors but lackluster teammates. Of course, the ones at the back of the pack had no chance either. So who did? The ones in the middle of the pack, who took nothing for granted and learned to work hard for what they had. These are the ones who do the little things well and spend extra time studying, working out, and seeking to find any advantage they could.

Recruiting and Interviewing

The recruiting process begins with creating an understanding of what the organization needs, in the form of a position description, and putting it out on the street. We think of the resumes that come in as nothing more than a foot in the door. Resumes don't answer the question of "Will they do the job?" or "Will they fit in?" but they give you a first indication of whether they can do the job and a basis for prioritizing candidates.

We develop our answers to the three questions through the interviewing process.

Can they do the job? That's straightforward. Do they have the expertise, the education, the experience, the training required to do the job? If it's a graphic designer and we use Adobe Illustrator, have they used the program? If the answer is no, but they've used InDesign, they're not that far apart; can we train them in Illustrator?

Will they do the job? This one's a lot harder to discern in an interview; the true answer may not reveal itself for several months. You're trying to assess their work ethic and their fit as a team player. We might pose a scenario in the interview that tells them something about our expectations while telling us something about them too: we have a project that's due tomorrow, you've worked fifty hours already this week, and now you're looking at an all-nighter; how are you going to handle that? But the closest we can come to getting a real answer in the interviewing process is to give them a task as a test. If it's a graphic designer, we might ask them to produce a PowerPoint presentation showing how they'd make three pages on our website better. Do they get it done? Are they proud of what they show you? How do they respond to feedback and criticism? At

Boulder Crest, a lot of people are attracted to helping veterans and first responders, and will tell you how much they want to be a part of the organization. But in what ways are they showing you that this is true? Do they come having researched the organization in detail and with an understanding of what we do? Do they create their own tasks to bring to the interview to show initiative but also passion for the task? One recent hire for an analyst position did precisely that; he showed up for his interview having already developed a data model for discussion, and even had it professionally printed on large, laminated pages.

Are they a good fit? Good fit relates to your culture, and culture is the way your organization gets things done. Their response to constructive criticism and challenging questions is a good first indicator. Do they show entrepreneurial tendencies? Bureaucratic? How do their core values align with yours as an organization? Selflessness is one of our core values at Boulder Crest; is there volunteer work in their background? Integrity is another one of our core values; we might ask how they made amends for something they did wrong in life. We'll dig as deeply into their background as we can. Have they been arrested for DUI? Gone into bankruptcy? Did they fail to disclose those things in the interview?

And of course, even when we answer the three questions to our satisfaction, we still don't always get it right. Neither will you; no leader can.

That's why, when you do get it wrong, you need to get the person you've brought on to your team off it as quickly as you can.

GETTING THE RIGHT PEOPLE IN THE RIGHT SEATS

There's debate over this, but at the end of the day most people believe in something like the 80/20 or 90/10 rule when it comes to employees. Twenty percent of your people take up 80 percent of your time, very likely because they're struggling—professionally, personally, or in both arenas. Or it's 90/10, however you choose to think of it. And on the other hand, 20 percent of the employees accomplish 80 percent of the work. As leaders, the problem is that we spend the majority of our time absorbed by the minority of people who are the least productive. Whether right or wrong, that's a common dynamic.

Let's step back to my definition of leadership: helping people get to a place they can't get to on their own. What does that mean, practically, with that 20 percent?

The first question to ask is whether you've put them in the wrong position. I believe that at the core of most people is goodness. My instinct is always to hope for the best. I begin by asking if there's more we can do to support someone who is struggling. Is it a matter of training? Is there a better fit for them within your organization? As the author Jim Collins put it, you've got to get the right people in the right seats on the bus. (Jim's book *Good to Great* is one of the best books I've read on business leadership.)

But as I've gained experience, I've also come to recognize that you can't let problems fester. If you try and there isn't a better fit, if they simply don't share the organization's core values, then you've got to get the struggling employee off the bus. I mentioned one of the concepts taught at Harvard Business School earlier in this chapter, and here's a second: hire slow, fire fast. At the end of the day, it's hard to get people to change—and leaders need to face that.

I operate with a three-strike philosophy. Of course, there are some behaviors that don't warrant a second strike. But we are human; none of us are perfect. In all but the most egregious cases, we deserve the chance to learn from our mistakes, and for others, to forgive and accept. That's consistent with the science of Posttraumatic Growth: when something knocks you down, you've got to pick yourself up, dust yourself off, and figure out how to move forward with resolve and fortitude.

In the end, though, the individual isn't all that matters; it's also about the organization and how others perceive and accept the mistakes someone has made. As a small organization, our resources are limited, and the consequences of a misfit are considerable. You can't neglect the people who are making the organization successful by burdening them with work that someone else was hired to do. Otherwise, you'll eventually break the backs of even your strongest workers because they'll reach a point where they're no longer satisfied with your leadership—and leave.

I've talked about the importance of "do as I do" leadership, of holding yourself accountable to others as their leader. People stick with leaders like that. But if you write a manual that describes your organization's core values and fail to live up to them yourself, by failing to ensure that others meet your expectations, that's transparent. People begin to wonder, what is it exactly that will get me fired? As their leader, you'll find yourself being held accountable for your own failures and undermining the organization and culture you set out to build.

> **Getting the right people on the team and in the right positions is central to a leader's success.**

CHAPTER 7

LEAD WELL #7

Create a Culture of Loyalty and Satisfaction

"Satisfaction is a rating. Loyalty is a brand."

—Shep Hyken

Whor we sold A-T Solutions, every one of the thirteen business partners made a lot of money. Because my wife and I owned the majority of the company, we made the most—but every one of the partners became a multi-millionaire. We had earned it, all of us, the hard way, building the company together from its start in my garage, leaping from fifty employees to 500 in just a few short years. We all put in hard work over long hours because we were building something we believed in. There was a time when I would have called the other shareholders my eleven best friends.

The decision to sell took a majority vote of the shareholders; my wife and I had no more weight than anyone else in that vote. I told the others that I thought we were selling a year or two early because of new projects in the pipeline that would increase the value of our company. But we were outvoted, ten to three.

The story of that sale sits heavy with me. I know there was a lot of jealousy around the fact that my wife and I made more than the others did. Our plan had been to sell the company from the beginning, and I stayed on for two more years before leaving to get my master's degree. I thought I had done a good job of explaining my goals, but when I left, my business partners felt that I'd abandoned them—even though they were the ones who had voted to sell the company.

I have no regrets about my vote—but my guess is that the partners who voted to sell live with a lot of regrets. Several of them are broke today. The stress of building the company took a toll on all of us, and though the company was filled with happy employees committed to shared core values, that was no longer the case for the shareholders. For them, in the end, the decision came down to the money. I remember thinking, in the room that day, that the one thing that allowed me to live with the decision to sell the company I founded was that I knew I didn't want to be in business with those ten partners any longer.

Today, I've completely lost touch with most of my former partners. For me, that reality is gut-wrenching.

I tell that difficult story to highlight Lead Well #7: *Create a culture of loyalty and satisfaction.* It shows how fragile building such a culture can be—and how important it is for a leader, even in the strongest organization, to cultivate it continuously. The work never ends.

THE FOUR QUADRANTS
OF LOYALTY AND SATISFACTION

While I was participating in the Harvard Business School Executive Education Program, I took a class in customer service with Frances X. Frei, the author of *Uncommon Service.* She taught an approach to putting customers first that began with plotting where they fell in four quadrants defined by their loyalty to your brand on one axis and their satisfaction on the other. A customer high on satisfaction might buy a $5 loaf of your bread every day, but if they were low on loyalty and another bakery opened down the street and sold $4 bread, they'd jump ship in a heartbeat, no matter how much they liked your bread. Frei believed your approach to customers should be influenced by where they fell on the quadrant, and your goal as a business was to move or attract more customers to the high loyalty, high satisfaction quadrant.

I approached her after class and asked if I could apply the same approach to my employees. "Absolutely," she said. "That's the corporate culture. I'm teaching the customer culture and customer behavior model here, but that's the corporate culture and behavior model."

So I applied it, thinking about where I'd place my employees in the four quadrants. It was illuminating. I've since adapted her approach; the names I've given to the four quadrants are mine, by and large, but the underlying concept is hers. She wouldn't recognize some of these terms, though!

Let's go through the quadrants and the characteristics that define them one by one.

Terrorists

Low Loyalty, Low Satisfaction, and actively destructive.

Maybe they like building and planting bombs. Maybe they'd rather hunt elephants in Africa. They take satisfaction in being destructive, in living in a world of terror—and they'd do it for anybody.

They're not motivated by loyalty to a cause, so their cause may change. They're angry and reactive, and they're going to act in anger, often.

Their influence on your organization is, like their mindset, destructive. Nothing good can come of their presence. With terrorists, your approach is pretty simple: they have to go.

Mercenaries

Low Loyalty, High Satisfaction, and looking out for themselves.

I had two employees at A-T Solutions who spent a year or so with us, learned everything we had to offer, then left to start their own business with our curriculum. On their way out the door they downloaded 30,000-some documents off our SharePoint drive.

Mercenaries are me-first, egocentric thinkers. Not necessarily unhappy in their job or destructive while they hold it, but low on loyalty.

They may reveal themselves in the hiring process because mercenaries are the most likely to push for more pay and more benefits during the hiring process than the position you're filling offers. Once they're on board, no matter what you do for them, it's not enough. No matter how well-suited they are to their role, at the next better job offer, they'll bolt.

Mercenaries are best avoided too, but they are not beyond hope. They are high on one end of the scale; can you move them in the right direction on the other?

Captives

High Loyalty, Low Satisfaction, and committed to you, not the work itself.

You could think of captives as friends who are loyal to you as an individual, but not satisfied in their job. My former business partners are good examples of captives: loyal but no longer satisfied with their work or the mission. A tough dynamic. They may have been with you for twenty years, but they've reached the point where they hate coming into work in the morning because they no longer want to take the next unhappy phone call, angry email, or employee complaint—whatever it may be. They're not going anywhere, necessarily, but they're no longer satisfied with what they're doing. Maybe they are just in it for the money?

Captives are not beyond hope either, but they are in need of your leadership.

Apostles

High Loyalty, High Satisfaction, and where you want everyone on your team to be.

God bless them. They lift your organization to success in fulfilling its mission. Reward them, recognize them, and hold them up as examples for others to see.

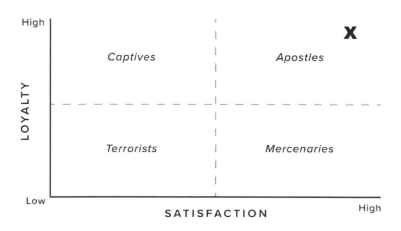

WHAT THE QUADRANTS
MEAN FOR LEADERS

Characteristics such as loyalty and satisfaction are difficult to measure, but if you create a scale of one to five or one to ten along each axis and begin to place people where they fall in your mind, you create a picture of your corporate culture as a whole, as well as seeing where you need to focus your efforts. There are other ways to analyze people and organizations, but I've found this way of thinking to be a useful tool in clarifying the work I should be doing to bring out the best in every person I'm leading.

The more you know the people who work for you, the more you know how to work with them. It goes back to my definition of leadership: helping people get to a place they can't get to on their own.

I value loyalty—not necessarily to me, but to the organization's mission—very highly. If I observe someone slipping from Apostle to Captive, still loyal to the cause but no longer satisfied in their job, then maybe I've got them in the wrong seat on the bus. They may need nothing more than a different opportunity within the organization. I might approach them by saying, "I appreciate your loyalty, but I can see you're not satisfied with your job. What can we do? Is there anything else here that would change that, or can I help you go somewhere else where you'll feel more satisfied in your work?"

If I have somebody who's highly satisfied in their job but not necessarily loyal to the cause—a mercenary—then I might spend more time with them in an effort to build a stronger personal relationship. As the saying goes, trust builds relationships, and relationships build loyalty.

And a terrorist? If I'm not dealing with their presence by moving them out, that's a failure on my part as a leader.

I go through this exercise all the time in my mind. Where does this person fall in the four quadrants? Where do we as an organization stand collectively? What am I going to do today to foster an organization of apostles?

I return to this theme at every leadership meeting too: think about our customers, think about our donors, think about our employees and where they fit on this chart.

That's where your leadership activity has to be focused, developing and guiding your employees to the place where they're *great* employees. Great employees make a great company, not the other way around. It's not a chicken and egg dynamic; success begins with fostering a culture defined by great employees.

The role of a leader is to work individually
with others to get them to a better place—
if not with you, somewhere else.

CHAPTER 8

LEAD WELL #8

Hold Yourself and Others Accountable

*"No person can be a great leader unless he takes genuine
joy in the successes of those under him."*

—W.H. Auden

In 1989, I was severely injured in a parachute jump in Puerto
Rico. We were not supposed to jump in winds higher than
eight knots unless it was a combat situation. They put us out that
day in gusts over thirty-five knots. I hit the ground hard—feet,
ass, and head instead of feet-side-shoulder—and broke my back,
dislocated my shoulder, and got a severe concussion.

The following week a good friend of mine died in another parachute jump. He had been among the guys out drinking heavily the night before. His main chute failed, and by the time he realized he needed to pull his reserve chute, he was on top of the trees. It was too late.

The nature of the two incidents is different. But together they illustrate the importance of Lead Well #8: *Hold yourself and others accountable.*

As leaders, when we fail to learn from our mistakes, to hold ourselves and others accountable for actions and their results, the consequences spread like a virus. Poor performance and even destructive behavior become the norm. Doing the wrong thing is okay. The results can cripple your organization.

I'm not talking only about life and death matters. Imagine two workers. The first shows up on time every day, sits right down, and begins to work. The other walks in twenty minutes late every day —and then goes to get a cup of coffee in the break room and chats with others in there. They're both getting the same paycheck. What message does that send? How long before the good worker begins doing the same thing? Or leaves, disillusioned, for another job in a better environment?

The biggest reason leaders struggle with accountability is the fear of how the conversation may go. Accountability isn't just about negative behavior. As a leader you need to reward positive behavior too. In many organizations, accountability means a bonus plan for individual and collective success. In any organization, it means promotions and public recognition for high achievers who demonstrate leadership themselves.

RESPONSIBILITY AND ACCOUNTABILITY

People tend to confuse responsibility and accountability. Most people want responsibility but not accountability. Responsibility is about duty and control over tasks and others. More responsibility brings higher pay and prominence in an organization. Accountability is about an individual or a group experiencing consequences, good or bad, for their actions. Most people find that an uncomfortable proposition. They avoid risk and resist measurement—but seek responsibility just the same, usually for status and money.

The difference between responsibility and accountability isn't revealed until something goes wrong. That's when everybody starts pointing fingers. It's his fault; it's her fault; it's not our fault. Finger-pointing is contagious too.

The job of a leader is to make deliverables clear and measurable, and ensure that those responsible for achieving them are held accountable for the results—positively or negatively, as the case may be. A finger-pointer is demonstrating to the leader that they're not truly committed to the level of responsibility they hold. They may be a good mechanic, fully capable of fixing the generators in your engine room. But they shouldn't be responsible for the engine room and the others in it because they don't understand what that requires. They're not willing to hold themselves accountable, so those they're leading won't hold themselves or each other accountable either. Building an accountable organization provides teammates with the ability to stand up for themselves and confront each other head on.

Brushing problems under the rug is another form of avoiding accountability; let's just pretend that didn't happen. In Chapter 1, on leading from wellness, I told the story of the Navy officer who held the Bible aloft at his change of command ceremony and thanked Jesus for his success—only to be arrested two weeks later for soliciting a prostitute. My commander—his boss—made matters worse by letting it slide. He told me that he didn't want to ruin the officer's career, that no one else would find out what he had done. But of course, they did. And they also knew that if it had been a junior officer or an enlisted troop, the commander would have come down on them like a ton of bricks.

WHAT ACCOUNTABILITY MEANS
FOR A LEADER

As a leader, I'm harder on myself than anybody else. I set a standard for myself that is very difficult for others to meet because I believe that you lead by example. To me, accountability means that when I screw up, I acknowledge it openly and we have a conversation about it.

I insist that other leaders in the organization hold themselves accountable too. Every year at Boulder Crest, as a management team, we bring in a consultant to facilitate our two-day strategic planning conference, where we review everything from our vision to our business plan for the next three years and set specific goals for the year to come. (I talked about this in Chapter 3, on setting goals.)

At the end of that effort, everyone on the management team signs a paper saying that they are accountable for seeing that the plan is executed. In eleven years, we have had two managers leave as a result, both of their own accord.

One made a habit of coming to the monthly management meeting without having the work he was responsible for completed. Finally, another manager called him on it. An hour after that meeting, he walked into my office and resigned. "I'm just not organized enough to get this stuff done in the time that it needs to be done," he said.

The second instance came on the day after the annual strategic planning meeting. "I sat there for two days, and it all sounded exciting," that manager said. "But when I went home and started talking with my wife about the amount of time I'm working, we decided that the management team wasn't right for me."

I admired them both for holding themselves accountable. And I believe their stories show the value in a culture built—beginning at the top—around accountability.

THE POSITIVE SIDE OF ACCOUNTABILITY

I'll admit it: I'm terrible at acknowledging good work. I grew up with a dad who gave us chores, and one of them was cutting the grass. He taught us how to do it properly and then expected us to do it right. If he came home and the lines weren't straight, we'd hear about it. But he never came home and said, "Oh, great job cutting the grass!" He gave you a job, and he expected the lines to be straight.

I'm better at acknowledging a job well done than my dad was, but I'm not as good as I should be. It's funny because in the military I was always prouder of my unit awards than my individual awards. I'm not alone in that; recipients of the military's highest award, the

Medal of Honor, never want to talk about what they did. They talk about what their unit did. (On the other hand, there are people who put themselves in for awards. There's a lot of me, me, me everywhere.)

Accountability is a two-way street, with positive consequences running in one direction and negative consequences running in the other. They're equally important.

At Boulder Crest, we have a young grant writer who cranked out fifteen grant applications in two weeks. The normal pace is one or two grants a month. When I realized that her above-and-beyond performance had gone unnoticed, I made a point of seeking her out and thanking her. And I'm honest with people. This doesn't come naturally to me, so if I don't pat you on the back, I want you to understand why. Being better at that remains high on my list for self-improvement.

> **Effective leaders take ownership for the outcomes, good or bad, of their decisions and hold others to the same standard.**

CHAPTER 9

LEAD WELL #9

Lead with Courage

*"Often the difference between a
successful person and a failure is not one has
better abilities or ideas, but the courage that
one has to bet on one's ideas, to take a
calculated risk—and to act."*

—Andre Malraux

The definition of courage is not the absence of fear. In fact,
the definition of courage is the opposite: the ability to do
something that frightens you. To lead with courage, you have to
have the confidence to stare your fears in the face—from something

95

as simple as speaking in public to crawling on your hands and knees to clear a minefield. Courage is the characteristic that separates good leaders from great leaders. Courage is also one of the hardest skills to teach in a book because courage requires experience and failures!

As a bomb disposal person, you're so highly trained that it tends to minimize the fear. The fear rises when you're faced with something you weren't trained to do—but it's still the training and experience that enables you to face it. Clearing a minefield in daylight with the proper equipment where the location of the mines is clearly identifiable is much different than lying on your belly in darkness, wearing night vision goggles, with no clue how the minefield might have been laid and working as quickly as you can because there are people behind you who need to get somewhere fast. You couldn't do either of these tasks without the training.

I tell that story to illustrate the importance of Lead Well #9: *Lead with courage.*

As a leader, fears come to you at different times and in different ways. How you face them and take them on is most important for your own confidence and building the confidence of your teammates. The consequences may be different from one time to the next, but the challenge of facing your fears stays the same. Perhaps you've heard the saying: "Every public speaker has butterflies in their stomach. The great ones teach them to fly in formation." Teams that understand this formation—their vision as an organization—are unstoppable.

That captures the essence of the belief system we taught in *Struggle Well*. As humans, we are the product of our training and our environment; the more you train and the more experience you gain, the easier it becomes to stare your fears in the face and ultimately find your true north. Moral strength and integrity are keys to courageous behaviors.

Effective leaders take calculated risks based in their training and experience. Understanding the risk enables you to face it head on. Managing risk actually requires you to be comfortable with who you are and take the appropriate actions required. Courage shows most clearly when things change and you face the need to call on your training, adapt, and take a risk beyond what you'd normally accept. Courage and boldness in decision-making inspires teammates and allows organizations to tackle the hardest of problems and create transformative change. Courageous leaders inspire teams to face and overcome their fears and succeed.

COURAGE AND VULNERABILITY

You can't have courage without vulnerability—that is, an awareness of the downside of risk and the harm that can come from failure. That sense of vulnerability is the source of fear. But you can have vulnerability without courage—and that leads to the inability to face your fears, which as a leader will leave you overwhelmed and paralyzed. As individuals and as a culture, we get in trouble when we separate courage from vulnerability. Authentic vulnerability helps to build trust among team members. The more trust that you have in an organization, the more support you will receive.

Again, whether the consequences are large or small, the dynamic is the same. When I approach a team member and acknowledge that I'm not great at giving pats on the back, I'm showing vulnerability and courage at the same time.

One of the reasons we do what we do at Boulder Crest is because I met many mental health professionals who I didn't think were healthy enough to take care of combat veterans who had been forged on the battlefield. They were just too vulnerable to help these vets, who found themselves scarred in ways that left them vulnerable as well. There's an element of tough love in the programs we run at Boulder Crest because we believe it's necessary to re-instill veterans with the courage they need to face their challenges.

MANAGING RISK

The definition of risk is exposure to danger, and when we dive into a swimming pool, there's always at least a little risk involved. If the water is shallow, you can break your neck. Fear of getting into water is natural, especially if you haven't been trained to swim. Diving into water is risky because there are potential dangers lurking under the surface. Understanding the depth of the water and acting accordingly is risk management: controlling the probability of an unfortunate event.

If we dive into water without knowing its depth, that's reckless. So is diving into water knowing that it is only three feet deep. But if we understand that the water is only three feet deep and choose to jump in feet first instead of dive, then we have faced our fear, managed our risk, and still gotten ourselves in the water.

Taking risks is a leader's responsibility—and so is risk management. If you separate the two, you are asking for trouble.

There are layers of risk in almost every decision: second- and third-order consequences of the decisions we make. A leader needs to be aware of these too. If I'm debating between jumping or diving into water and I can't swim, then I should be worrying more about learning to swim than how I'm going to get in the water.

A good leader asks more than one question before taking a risk. They ask, what's the immediate unfortunate event I need to manage, and then what are the other unfortunate events that could happen because of my decision-making?

THE IMPORTANCE OF COMMITMENT

Courage requires commitment: seeing things through to the end. Leaders who jump from thing to thing to thing without seeing any of them through create an organizational culture that emulates that tendency.

That's why it is so important to define a goal, see it through, check it off, celebrate it—and move on to the next thing.

I'm not saying you can't do multiple things at once, like walking and chewing gum. What I am saying is that everything your organization takes on needs to be seen through to the end—and your responsibility as a leader is to ensure that happens. Seeing something through to the end does not mean you do so at all costs; recognizing failure or changing circumstances and making a clear decision to stop takes courage too.

A waffling leader is incapable of facing their fear, assessing their risk, and stepping off; if a leader is willing to step off but doesn't see things through, that's another form of waffling leadership. In either case, their behavior is sure to proliferate throughout the organization. Everybody sees it, sees that you're okay with it, and assumes it's okay for them too. Courage builds amazing collaborative teams and a capacity for taking risks.

> An effective leader demonstrates the ability
> to see risks clearly, manages their consequences,
> and celebrates their win and failures.

CHAPTER 10

LEAD WELL #10

Give Back

*"A Spiritual Samaritan lives knowing that if
we were to leave this world tomorrow, we were the best
humans we could be and we touched the lives of as many
souls as possible. We are not asked to be perfect.
We are asked to make a difference."*

—Molly Friedenfeld

The importance of giving back has been ingrained in me
since I was a very young boy. I grew up in a faithful Cath-
olic family. My grandparents and parents were community-first
examples of taking care of your neighbors and those less fortu-
nate, whether it was giving in the offertory basket at church or

volunteering in the kitchen to provide food baskets at Thanksgiving. Giving has always been an important part of my life.

The Navy reinforced that with its own giving campaigns and the message its best leaders sent: find a passion and a cause greater than yourself and embrace it. When I was stationed in Maryland, we prepared Thanksgiving dinners for civilian families living just outside the base; while stationed in Scotland, I played for a hockey team that raised money for a local hospice.

I tell these stories to illustrate Lead Well #10: *Give back.* When you engage in these activities, performing acts of kindness, you gain perspective on what really matters in life—and at least in a small way, make the world a better place too. I believe it's a central element of leading from spiritual wellness.

Boulder Crest emerged from this philosophy.

In 2004, early in the war on terror, my wife and I started a charity known today as the EOD Warrior Foundation. In the course of supporting severely wounded bomb disposal personnel undergoing treatment at the Walter Reed National Military Hospital complex in Bethesda, Maryland, we began bringing their families out to our farm in Bluemont, Virginia, for barbecues. A few stayed with us over weekends—but when people are in your home, no matter how welcoming you are, they always feel like guests.

In 2010, we decided to donate thirty-seven acres of our estate and millions of dollars to build what became the first Boulder Crest Retreat. Our idea was to provide families with a home away from home, a respite from the hospital about an hour away. We built four log cabins there, a fishing pond and playground, a lodge, a walled garden, an archery range, a labyrinth, a treehouse, and walking trails, with horses in the back pasture. We opened officially as a nonprofit in 2013. Three years later, we received a large gift and opened a second facility in Arizona.

Today, about 1,500 veterans, first responders, and family members come through our gates every year to participate in our programs, along with another 1,500 or so volunteers and event-goers.

WHY JUST COMING TO WORK ISN'T ENOUGH

When a leader sets an example by giving back, others follow, and the result is much more than a matter of checking a box. The fulfilling feeling that results from giving back creates a sense of purpose in our lives and stretches our compassion beyond our immediate clan.

In *Struggle Well*, we shared our philosophy of concentric circles of healing: you have an obligation to be well to yourself first, then to help your family, your friends, and then your community. The circles don't stop there either; they can extend to the nation and the global community if your desires lead you there.

Why bring this philosophy into the workplace? Because I believe that it adds a sense of purpose to the lives of everyone who works there. Even at Boulder Crest, where everything we do is ultimately philanthropic, our employees volunteer at women's abuse shelters, animal shelters, and drug and alcohol treatment centers—some open their homes as foster parents. We believe that even people who do charitable work need to get out of that frame of reference to explore something bigger. Challenges exist in every community in the United States—including Loudoun County, where I live, the richest county in the country—and it's important that we're all exposed to them. Drug abuse, drug dealing, gangs, domestic violence, homelessness, hunger—they happen everywhere.

THE TWO FORMS OF GIVING BACK

I believe there are two forms of giving back. The first I'd call charitable giving, and the second philanthropic giving.

Charitable giving is focused on addressing a crisis—the suffering that's caused by social problems. For people who are homeless, providing them with a home. For the hungry, a meal. For those in danger, a safe shelter.

Philanthropic giving addresses broader societal problems. It gets to the deepest of our human needs. We have a homeless population; we need a great work program and more housing in our community, and then more industries providing more and better jobs.

Each of these is important. But our time and, for most of us, our finances are limited; how and toward which end do you want to spend what you can of both? Where do your passions lie?

As you look for organizations to support, remember that research shows that in the world of nonprofit giving, people tend to give to people. That means givers want to believe in the leaders of the organizations they're supporting—to give in whatever form with the confidence that not only is your giving appreciated but that it's being properly used. You don't want to be involved in organizations that misuse the precious resources they receive.

THE THREE WAYS TO BE
A PHILANTHROPIST

Again, when I speak of philanthropy, I'm talking about improving the wellbeing of humankind. I think there are three ways to be a philanthropist.

The first form of philanthropy is sharing a nonprofit's message. Thanks to social media, this is easier today than ever before. When you see something that inspires you, cheer it on. Share it to your network. You never know where it might lead. I once trained an EOD student in the Navy back in 1994. He went on to do well, and when his father died, he left the service to run the family business. I hadn't seen him since EOD school. Then we connected on Facebook. He was inspired by our work and introduced me to his brother. One day his brother called me to say that he was a lawyer with a client in Maryland who was interested in giving some of his wealth away to help veterans; could he bring the client by? Not only has his client become a friend, he has donated well over a million dollars to our organization.

The second form of philanthropy is volunteering inside an organization. At Boulder Crest we have volunteers in our kitchens who wash dishes for our programs; in animal shelters, there are volunteers who simply wash beds, towels, and toys. They're not necessarily difficult tasks, but they're very meaningful to an organization because time is money. Even if you volunteer and find you don't connect with the work a nonprofit does, seeing what they do and how they do it might help you direct your time to the right causes in the future.

The third and most obvious form of philanthropy is giving money. Every nonprofit that's doing socially responsible work is in need of money because they're almost all privately funded. It may not be the most important thing to the organization, but money is always needed.

DEMONSTRATING GENEROSITY

As a leader, when you do something, or foster it, it's contagious. There are many people who give or volunteer anonymously, and that's great. But when you do it openly—or publicly acknowledge others who do—the spirit spreads. We recognize our dish-washing volunteers at every program by bringing them in front of the participants to thank them. There are corporations that bring fifty or sixty people to Boulder Crest to tackle bigger projects, such as painting our horse pasture fences or mulching our flower beds. Working side by side with others creates a contagion of giving back.

THE PURPOSE OF MONEY

I have never been motivated by money. Financially speaking, I think the goal is to do good things in life, work hard, and make the right investments so that you can retire one day without worrying about having enough resources to carry you to the end of life.

I believe the more money you have, the more problems you have. Rich people's problems don't go away; rich people have rich people's problems. They wreck more expensive cars, they buy more expensive houses, their kids do more expensive drugs. More money doesn't solve their problems. It just creates different ones.

The people who are, in fact, blessed with money have an obligation to ensure that it goes beyond the walls of their house. That's the difference between a life and a life with purpose. My dad used to say that the only things you truly leave behind on Earth when you die are your children and your reputation.

FOSTERING A CULTURE OF GIVING

At Boulder Crest, we don't require volunteer work, but we reward it. When COVID-19 hit, we were forced to shut down our facility for six weeks while we figured out what we needed to do to run our programs in a pandemic. In that time, I challenged our employees to go do something for the community. Our mission is to teach the science of Posttraumatic Growth to individuals; I encouraged the staff to look at it from an organizational perspective. What could we do to grow from this? Internally, in terms of fundraising or marketing or program improvements—but externally too. What could we do to help the community around us in a time of crisis?

Our employees in both Virginia and Arizona took that challenge to heart and did some amazing food and toilet paper drives for local food banks. It fostered a culture across the organization of doing more for others—a culture of giving back.

I've talked earlier about studies showing that 70 percent of Americans in the workforce hate their jobs. As leaders of organizations, we have to create an environment where there's meaning in every task, whether it's emptying the trash baskets or putting the next satellite in space, and to tie every task back to our vision and our mission. When people share a sense of purpose, their morale rises. Researchers have found that their mental and physical health can improve too.

By demonstrating and encouraging community engagement, leaders also boost morale. They show that they and the organization itself believe in a greater purpose, not just in terms of personal responsibility but corporate responsibility too—and that creates an environment where people don't run from their work. They run to it.

> We all share an obligation to ensure that our neighbors in life are taken care of. Effective leaders embrace their greater responsibility to others and set an example through volunteering and giving.

CONCLUSION

"Cynicism is just cowardice. It is nothing less than a form of surrender."

—Secretary of Defense Jim Mattis

I once served a two-year exchange tour in England with the Royal Navy, where I worked with a Chief who was fond of repeating a saying: *When you leave the Navy, it's like putting your hand in a bucket of water and pulling it out. After the water settles, nobody knows that you were ever there.*

I found that to be so cynical. Finally, after the fifth or sixth time I heard him say it, I replied. "You know, Chief, I just don't agree with your philosophy."

"Well, let me show you," he said.

"No," I said, "you don't have to show me. I understand your analogy, but I believe that every Sailor, every Soldier, every Marine, and every Airman that we train, we leave an imprint on. They may forget your name and your face as they go on, but that imprint will make or break them on the battlefield and in their lives."

Great leaders aren't cynical and don't think of themselves as a hand in a bucket of water. They look at the opportunity we all have to leave an imprint on others.

There are thousands of books on leadership. And many of them might tell you that the principles of effective leadership change with the times.

I disagree with that too. I believe that the basic principles of effective leadership never change. They persist from generation to generation because I believe that something else even more fundamental never changes either, that as human beings, we have two goals in life:

- The opportunity to contribute.

- The opportunity to grow.

Leadership is a verb. As I've said, I define leadership as helping others get to a place they can't get to on their own. And I believe that you can achieve that by following the Lead Well 10, the principles of leadership I've outlined in this book.

#1: Lead Yourself First

To lead others well, you need to lead yourself to wellness first.

#2: Set and Clearly Communicate Your Vision

Visions that don't serve as a real and meaningful guide to action will fail.

#3: Set and Achieve Goals that Align with Your Vision

Your vision leads naturally to your goals, and the true measure of hard work toward those goals is outcomes.

#4: Listen Well

Managers move paper, but leaders move people—and that begins by listening to them.

#5: Lead with Kindness

An effective leader says what they mean, means what they say—and doesn't act out of a spirit of meanness toward others.

#6: Hire Quality People

Getting the right people on the team and in the right positions is central to a leader's success.

#7: Create a Culture of Loyalty and Satisfaction

The role of a leader is to work individually with others to get them to a better place—if not with you, somewhere else.

#8: Hold Yourself and Others Accountable

Effective leaders take ownership for the outcomes, good or bad, of their decisions and hold others to the same standard.

#9: Lead with Courage

An effective leader demonstrates the ability to see risks clearly, manage their consequences, and take them on.

#10: Give Back

We all share an obligation to ensure that our neighbors in life are taken care of. Effective leaders embrace their greater responsibility to others and set an example through volunteering and giving.

Today the world needs great leadership as much as ever, if not more. May you be a leader, and may you Lead Well.

ACKNOWLEDGMENTS

You can't write a book without sacrificing time with those you love. First, I would like to thank my wife for her patience with my absence while I was deployed during my military service, on the road for business, on the phone, or behind a computer screen. Thank you, Julia; you are the rock of our family and the love of my life. To our beautiful daughters; Gennavieve and Rhian; my son-in-law, Brayden; and my four grandkids, Troy, Riley, Cameron, and Gwendolyn—Thank You. I will never get back the time spent away from you, and I hope to spend more time with you as I continue to grow old.

To all of those who led me (the good and the bad) along the way and to all of those who called me their leader. I am very grateful for the mutual inspiration and success that we shared.

And finally, to my dad. Your leadership and words of wisdom shaped my life. You made me the man I am, and I'll spend the rest of my life translating and sharing the lessons I learned from you. You are sorely missed, and I am grateful to live and share your legacy!

ABOUT THE AUTHOR

KEN FALKE spent twenty-one years in the US Navy as a bomb disposal specialist, leading troops on thousands of high-risk missions. After retiring from the Navy in 2002, Ken started his first company, A-T Solutions, a counter-terrorism company, and in 2008 sold the business. In 2011, Ken started his second company, Shoulder 2 Shoulder, and sold his stock to his business partner in 2017. In addition to Ken's two for-profit companies, he founded two nonprofit organizations, beginning with the EOD Warrior Foundation to support the families of severely wounded military bomb disposal personnel. This work inspired Ken and his family to donate thirty-seven acres of their estate in Bluemont, Virginia, and millions of dollars to build Boulder Crest Foundation in 2013—the nation's first privately funded wellness center dedicated exclusively to combat veterans, first responders, and their families—and go on to establish Boulder Crest Arizona and the Boulder Crest Institute for Posttraumatic Growth in 2017.